All about Me!

A Book by

_____

chronicle books · san francisco

Me

Here's a picture of me:

My **name** is Sion

This is my name because my mom gave me it

My **nicknames** are I don't have one

Right now I am ___happy___ feet, ___30___ inches tall.

I weigh _____ pounds.

The color of my **eyes** is ___brown___

I have **dimples** when I smile: ☐ Yes   ☐ No

Watch how fast you grow!
Use the height chart to measure and mark your height.

My Face
Draw and color in your eyes and hair. Add your dimples if you have them! Don't forget to draw the teeth you show when you smile!

My **hands** are this big:

I write with my ☐ left hand   ☑ right hand

Stickers to decorate your book!

Photo corners to hold your pictures.

Stickers to decorate your book!

My **thumb** is ____123____ inches long.

My **nose** is ____30____ inches long.

Use the ruler on the stencil to measure your body parts.

My **ears** are ____21____ inches long.

My **foot** is ____35____ inches long.

My **arm** is ____53____ inches long.

My **hand** is ____34____ inches long.

My **big toe** is ____31____ inches long and it looks like this:

I can

- [x] tie my shoes
- [ ] whistle
- [x] read a book
- [x] do 20 jumping jacks
- [x] make a silly noise
- [x] wiggle my toes
- [x] hum
- [x] count to 10
- [x] say the ABCs
- [x] skip
- [x] dance

My tummy is ticklish:

[x] Yes! [x] Not really.

Other places I am ticklish are

In my toes

I am

- [✓] silly
- [✓] honest
- [✓] caring
- [✓] friendly
- [✓] funny
- [✓] smart
- [✓] thoughtful
- [✓] shy
- [✓] loud
- [✓] adventurous
- [✓] helpful
- [✓] creative

When Magenta is being **silly**

she looks like this:

When I am being silly

I look like this:

The Nick Jr. character I am most like is

- [✓] Dora
- [ ] Blue
- [✓] Boots
- [ ] Joe
- [ ] Diego
- [ ] April
- [ ] Kiku
- [✓] Little Bill

I am like that character because

When I **grow up**, I want to be a

This is a picture of me when I grow up:

My Family and Friends

My **mom's** first name is

My **dad's** first name is

(But I call them _____ and _____ .)

I have _____ **brothers** and _____ **sisters**.

Their names are

Things we like to do together are

Make a Family Tree! Use the stencil to trace apples onto the tree, one for each member of your family. Use the big apple for the older people in your family and the smaller apple for the younger people. Write a name inside each of the apples. Decorate your tree with leaves, too!

My pet is a dog

My pet's name is nas

A **pet** I would like to have is a dog

If I had a **fish** it would look like this:

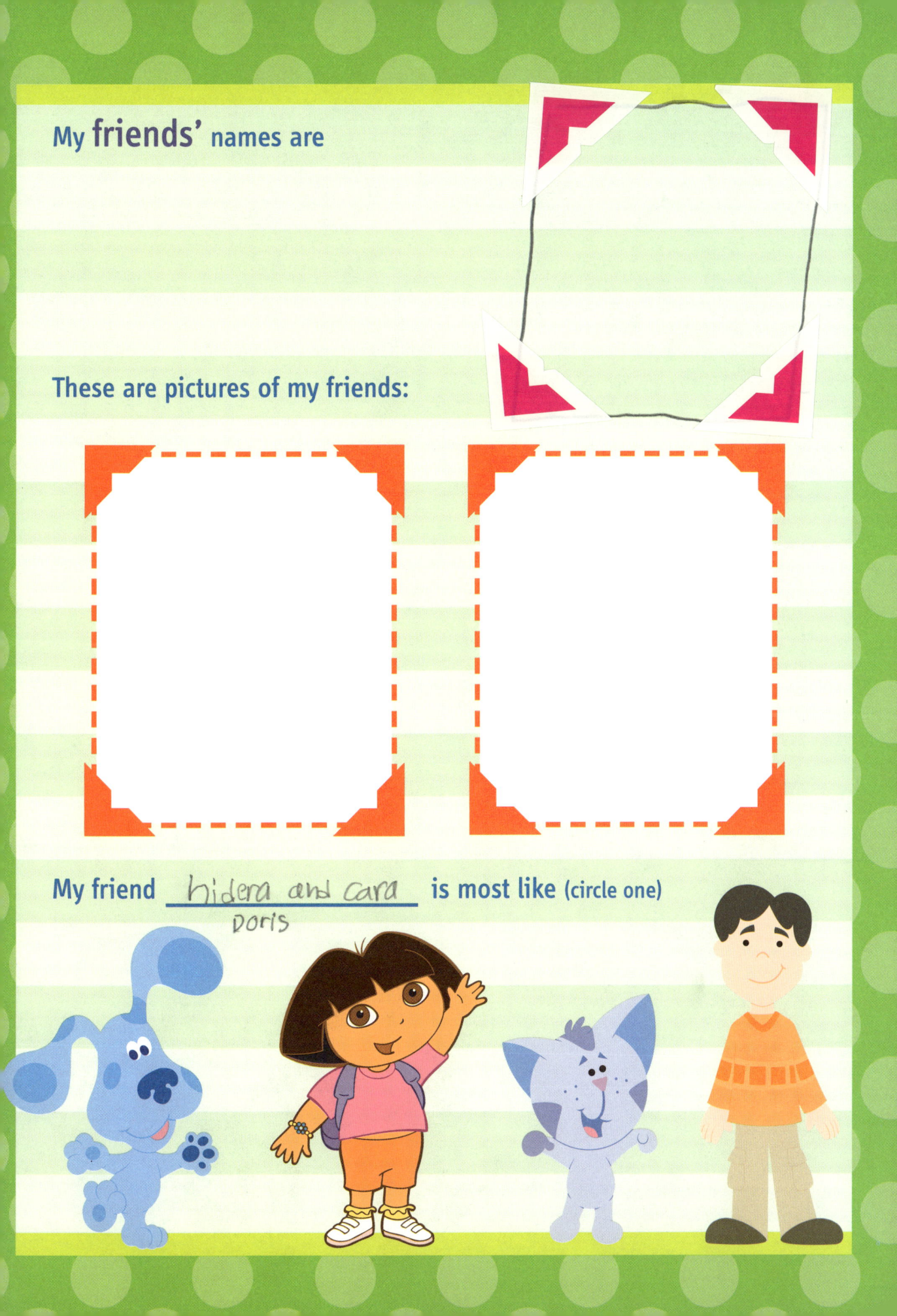

My friends' names are

These are pictures of my friends:

My friend _hidera and cara_ is most like (circle one)
             Doris

Things I like to do with my friends are

- [x] play outside
- [x] build forts
- [x] paint and draw
- [x] sing and dance
- [x] put on puppet shows
- [x] play games
- [x] watch movies
- [x] eat snacks
- [x] celebrate birthdays

My favorite thing to do with my friends is play outside

My **neighborhood** has a

- [x] school
- [x] grocery store
- [x] park or playfield
- [x] mailbox
- [x] stoplight or stop sign
- [ ] bank
- [ ] restaurant
- [ ] river or creek
- [ ] library
- [ ] bakery

The best place to play in my neighborhood is out side

The **state** I live in is now york

The **country** I live in is

My School

Here's a picture of me at school:

The name of my school is

I get to school by

- ☐ car
- ☐ bus
- ☐ my feet
- ☐ skateboard
- ☐ boat
- ☐ subway
- ☐ submarine
- ☐ hot-air balloon

Here's a picture of my **teacher** and **classmates**:

Here are their names:

Things I like to do at school are

- [ ] read books
- [ ] talk to friends
- [ ] listen to stories
- [ ] play inside
- [ ] play outside
- [ ] eat
- [ ] nap
- [ ] draw and paint
- [ ] sing and make music
- [ ] learn

These are things I eat at school:

Stencil with Your Pencil!

Use the stencil to practice writing letters and numbers.

For each letter of the **alphabet**, I can name something:

A is for

B is for

C is for

D is for

E is for

F is for

G is for

H is for

I is for

J is for

K is for

L is for

M is for

N is for

O is for

P is for

Q is for

R is for

S is for

T is for

U is for

V is for

W is for

X is for

Y is for

Z is for

My Birthday

I was **born** on ____1999____ at ____4____ o'clock.

I was born in Sante peters' hospital

I **weighed** __6lb 1oz__ pounds, __1__ ounces.

Here's a picture of me when I was born:

I will have this many **candles** on my next birthday cake:

Happy birthday Siong

On my **birthday** I like to

- [x] have a party
- [x] eat cake
- [x] open presents
- [x] play games
- [ ] watch magic tricks
- [x] sing songs
- [x] blow out candles
- [x] make a wish

My Vacation

Places I have been on vacation are

- [ ] beach
- [ ] mountain
- [ ] desert
- [x] amusement park
- [x] campsite
- [x] relative's house
- [x] big city
- [ ] farm or ranch
- [ ] zoo
- [ ] lake

This is the place I like to visit the most:

Greetings from the big city

Here's a picture of me on vacation:

Souvenirs I like to collect when I go places are

I like to travel most by (circle one)

My Feelings

When I feel happy I

- [x] smile
- [x] laugh
- [x] skip
- [x] hop
- [x] run
- [x] clap
- [x] giggle
- [x] twirl
- [x] flap my arms
- [x] hug someone
- [x] tell jokes
- [x] shout
- [x] dance
- [x] wiggle

When I feel tired I go to sleep

When I feel hungry I eat

When I feel mad I com down

These things make me happy when I feel sad:

hug some one

play

My Wishes

Here are four special wishes I have:

1
2
3
4

I like to make a wish when I

- ☐ toss a coin into a fountain
- ☐ find a four-leaf clover
- ☐ see a shooting star
- ☐ blow out birthday candles

What I Like

Foods I like to eat are

An **outfit** I like to wear is

A **game** I like to play is

A **song** I like to sing is

An **animal** I like to pet is

Nick Jr. characters I like are

A **movie** I like to watch is

A **place** I like to go is

A **book** I like to read is

A person I like to be is me!